Ace the CFE Exam

Comprehensive Practice Questions with Explained Answers

Knowledge Empire.

Question 1

How should a fraud examiner handle the collection of documents during an examination?

A. Wait until all documents have been collected before establishing a database

B. Organize all the documents obtained in chronological order

C. Whenever possible, avoid touching original documents

D. Make copies of originals and leave the originals where they were found

Correct Answer: C. Whenever possible, avoid touching original documents

Explanation: It is essential for a fraud examiner to minimize handling of original documents to preserve their integrity and avoid altering potential evidence. Touching original documents can potentially damage them or alter their appearance, which may impact the investigation's credibility and outcomes. Making copies of originals and leaving the originals where they were found helps maintain the integrity of the evidence and ensures that the investigation is conducted effectively.

Question 2

Why do fraud examiners analyze unstructured or textual data?

A. Analysis of data in order to identify patterns, sentiments, and relationships that indicate fraud

B. To find an admission of fraud in an email or other communication that can be presented in court

C. To figure out whether someone is lying or telling the truth based on contextual clues

D. To determine whether the footnotes to the financial statements are fairly presented

Correct Answer: A. Analysis of data in order to identify patterns, sentiments, and relationships that indicate fraud

Explanation: Analyzing unstructured or textual data allows fraud examiners to identify patterns, sentiments, and relationships that may indicate fraudulent activity. By categorizing and analyzing this type of data, examiners can uncover potential fraud schemes and gather evidence to support their findings.

Question 3

Which data analysis function is typically used to ensure that employee transactions comply with company policies, such as verifying that traveling employees book accommodations at approved hotels?

A. The Join function

B. The correlation analysis function

C. The compliance verification function

D. The gap testing function

Correct Answer: C. The compliance verification function.

Explanation: The compliance verification function is specifically designed to check whether transactions or actions comply with established rules or policies. It is often used to ensure that employees adhere to company guidelines, such as booking accommodations at approved hotels during travel.

Question 4

Which of the following actions can be considered a bribe, even if the actual illicit payment is never made?

A. Offering a payment
B. Corruption in payment
C. Kickback payment
D. Overbilling in payment

Correct Answer: A. Offering a payment.

Explanation: Offering a payment, even if the payment is not completed, can still be considered a bribe. The intent to offer a bribe is sufficient to constitute wrongdoing in many jurisdictions.

Question 5

In a jurisdiction where pretexting against financial institutions is prohibited, which of the following actions would be considered illegal pretexting?

A. Opening a bank account using a false identity
B. Pretending to be an account holder to view their bank records
C. Deliberately providing false information on loan applications
D. Stealing someone's mail to access their bank account number

Correct Answer: D. Stealing a person's mail to obtain their bank account number.

Explanation: Illegal pretexting involves using deceit or false pretenses to obtain information, such as accessing someone's bank account number by stealing their mail. This action is prohibited and punishable by law in many jurisdictions.

Question 6

Which of the following statements is NOT true regarding locating individuals using online records?

A. Before conducting a search, the fraud examiner should be aware of the most effective types of searches.

B. If an individual has moved, obtaining a past address is typically not helpful.

C. Online records are valuable for finding subjects whose locations are unknown.

D. When attempting to find a subject using internet records, the initial step should be to obtain the subject's previous address.

Correct Answer: D. When attempting to find a subject using internet records, the initial step should be to obtain the subject's previous address.

Explanation: While obtaining a past address can sometimes be helpful, it should not necessarily be the first step. The most effective approach may vary depending on the specific circumstances of the case.

Question 7

Naveed, a fraud suspect, has chosen to confess to Howard, a Certified Fraud Examiner (CFE). When obtaining a verbal confession from Naveed, Howard should gather all of the following details EXCEPT:

A. A general estimate of the amount of money involved.
B. A statement from Naveed claiming his conduct was accidental.
C. The approximate number of instances.
D. The location of any remaining assets.

Correct Answer: B. A statement from Naveed that his conduct was an accident.

Explanation: When obtaining a confession, it's important to gather information such as the amount of money involved, the number of instances, and the location of any remaining assets. However, whether the suspect claims their conduct was accidental is not relevant to the confession process.

Question 8

Which warning sign of check tampering could suggest that employees have misappropriated cash and recorded the theft as expenses?

A. Voided checks
B. Payable checks
C. Missing checks
D. Duplicate checks

Correct answer: C. Missing checks

Explanation: Missing checks could indicate that employees have stolen cash and recorded the theft as an expense, covering their tracks by removing the checks from the accounting records.

Question 9

What steps ought to be taken to get a company ready for an official fraud investigation?

A. Notify all managers about the investigation, explaining its purpose and the individuals involved.

B. Declare when the investigation is going to start and notify important decision-makers.

C. Send an email to all employees outlining the investigation's purpose.

D. Inform the subject that they are under investigation.

Correct Answer: B. Declare when the investigation is going to start and notify important decision-makers.

Explanation: It is important to inform key decision-makers within the organization when a formal fraud investigation is ready to begin to ensure that they are aware of the situation and can provide necessary support and guidance. However, notifying all managers, sending an email to all employees, or informing the subject under investigation should be done carefully and only as needed, based on the circumstances and the organization's policies.

Question 10

Which of the following steps should a fraud examiner NOT take when planning for the interview phase of an investigation?

A. Review the case file to ensure that no important information has been overlooked.

B. Consider the objective of the interview and state it clearly.

C. Prepare a brief outline of key points to discuss during the interview.

D. You should choose a venue where the subject will feel uncomfortable during the interview.

Correct Answer: D. You should choose a venue where the subject will feel uncomfortable during the interview.

Explanation: It is important for the interview to be conducted in a neutral and comfortable setting to encourage open communication and cooperation from the interviewee. Conducting the interview in a venue where the subject will feel uncomfortable can hinder the effectiveness of the interview.

Question 11

How is omitted credit detection primarily achieved in bookkeeping?

A. Forced Balance

B. Trend Analysis

C. Expense Account

D. None of the above

Correct Answer: A. Forced Balance

Explanation: Forced balance is the principal method for detecting omitted credits from books of account. It involves ensuring that all transactions are properly recorded to maintain a balanced account. Trend analysis, while useful for other purposes, is not specifically designed for detecting omitted credits. An expense account is a general ledger account used for recording all expenses incurred by a business. The correct answer, forced balance, is the most effective method for identifying discrepancies in the accounting records.

Question 12

What motivates individuals to engage in financial statement fraud?

A. To conceal false business performances

B. To preserve personal status

C. To maintain personal income

D. To stand outside the accounting system

Correct Answer: A. To conceal false business performances

Explanation: People commit financial statement fraud to conceal or misrepresent the true financial performance of a business. This can be done to attract investors, inflate stock prices, or secure loans under false pretenses. The other options may be motivations for fraud in general, but the primary reason for financial statement fraud is to deceive stakeholders about the true financial health of a company.

Question 13

What is a reason senior management might not overstate business statements?

A. To comply with debt covenants

B. To meet personal performance criteria

C. To trigger performance-related compensation

D. To show a pattern of growth to support the sale of a business

Correct Answer: A. To comply with debt covenants

Explanation: Senior management may overstate business statements for various reasons, such as meeting personal performance targets, triggering performance-related compensation, or showing a pattern of growth to support the sale of a business. However, complying with debt covenants typically requires accurate and truthful financial reporting, so it would not be a reason to overstate business statements.

Question 14

Which search is typically used to detect an unusually high incidence of returns and allowances scheme?

A. Allowances by vendors

B. Disposals of allowances than reorders

C. Returns and allowances

D. None of the above

Correct Answer: C. Returns and allowances

Explanation: The Returns and Allowances search is specifically designed to identify instances where there is an unusually high rate of returns or allowances, which could indicate fraudulent activity such as overstatement of returns to reduce income. The other options do not directly relate to detecting this type of scheme.

Question 15

What is the most common method of detecting corruption cases?

A. Internal audits

B. Internal controls

C. Tips

D. By accident

Correct Answer: C. Tips

Explanation: Tips, often from whistleblowers or anonymous sources, are the most common method of detecting corruption cases. While internal audits and controls are important for preventing and detecting fraud, tips are generally the initial trigger that leads to the discovery of corrupt activities. Detection by accident is less common than tips and usually occurs when irregularities are noticed unintentionally during routine activities.

Question 16

What term is used for undisclosed payments made by vendors to employees of purchasing companies?

A. Bid-rigging

B. Kickbacks

C. Presolicitation

D. None of the above

Correct Answer: B. Kickbacks

Explanation: Kickbacks are undisclosed payments or benefits provided to employees of a purchasing company by vendors in exchange for favorable treatment, such as being awarded contracts or making purchases from the vendor. Bid-rigging, on the other hand, involves conspiring to manipulate the bidding process to ensure a specific outcome, often to the detriment of fair competition. Presolicitation refers to activities or communications that occur before a formal solicitation or request for proposal is issued.

Question 17

Which process requires all bidders to be placed on the same plane of equality, bidding on the same terms and conditions?

A. Bid-rigging

B. Kickbacks

C. Competitive bidding

D. Bid solicitation

Correct Answer: C. Competitive bidding

Explanation: Competitive bidding is a process where organizations solicit bids from competing vendors to obtain goods or services. It is intended to ensure fairness and transparency by allowing all bidders to compete on the same terms and conditions. Bid-rigging, on the other hand, is an illegal practice where competitors conspire to manipulate the bidding process to ensure a specific outcome. Kickbacks involve undisclosed payments made to individuals in exchange for preferential treatment in bidding processes. Bid solicitation is the process of requesting bids from potential suppliers or contractors.

Question 18

Does a person's level of power over the bidding process correlate with their ability to influence the selection of a supplier?

A. True

B. False

Correct answer: A. True

Explanation: The more power a person has over the bidding process, the more likely they are to influence the selection of a supplier. This is because greater power can lead to more control and decision-making authority in the selection process.

Question 19

What characteristics are often seen in the behavior profile of employees involved in bribery schemes?

A. Gambling habit

B. Extravagant lifestyle

C. Drug and/or alcohol addiction

D. All of the above

Correct Answer: D. All of the above

Explanation: Employees involved in bribery schemes may exhibit a variety of behaviors, including gambling habits, living beyond their means (an extravagant lifestyle), and struggles with drug and/or alcohol addiction. These behaviors can sometimes be indicators of financial stress or attempts to fund a lifestyle beyond their legitimate means.

Question 20

What is the term for a scheme in which employees exploit their knowledge of their employer's intent to purchase a specific asset by purchasing it themselves?

A. Conflict of interest in sale

B. Turnaround sale or flip

C. Unauthorized sale

D. Written sale of unique assets

Correct Answer: B. Turnaround sale or flip

Explanation: A turnaround sale or flip occurs when employees take advantage of their knowledge about their employer's plan to purchase an asset by purchasing it themselves, often for the purpose of reselling it quickly for a profit. This behavior can raise ethical concerns and may constitute a conflict of interest.

Question 21

Which of the following terms describes long-lived assets that are distinct from property, plant, and equipment acquired through outright purchase or capital lease?

A. Tangible Assets

B. Intangible Assets

C. Forced Assets

D. None of the above

Correct Answer: B. Intangible Assets

Explanation: Intangible assets, such as patents, copyrights, trademarks, and goodwill, are assets without physical substance that have enduring value to a company. Tangible assets, on the other hand, are physical assets like property, plant, and equipment. Forced assets is not a recognized term in accounting or finance.

Question 22

How is a tangible asset defined?

A. Capable of being perceived

B. Capable of being appraised

C. Both A & B

D. Neither A nor B

Correct Answer: C. Both A & B

Explanation: A tangible asset is one that can be physically touched or perceived and can also be appraised or valued. This includes assets like machinery, equipment, buildings, and land, which have physical substance and can be evaluated in monetary terms.

Question 23

What term describes the practice of matching all expenses used to produce income consistently against that income?

A. Equity

B. Accrual basis accounting

C. Expense

D. Financial record

Correct Answer: B. Accrual basis accounting

Explanation: Accrual basis accounting is a method where expenses are recorded when they are incurred, regardless of when the payment is made. This means that expenses are matched against the income they help generate in a consistent manner, providing a more accurate representation of a company's financial position.

Question 24

True or False: Depreciation is particularly relevant when companies attempt to inflate their assets and overall worth; the less they record for depreciation, the greater their reported profits.

A. True

B. False

Correct Answer: A. True

Explanation: Depreciation is a method used to allocate the cost of a tangible asset over its useful life. Companies that want to appear more profitable may try to minimize their depreciation expenses, which could lead to an overvaluation of their assets and net worth on the balance sheet. This can artificially inflate profits because lower depreciation expenses result in higher reported profits.

Question 25

What term is used for expenses that are incurred but not yet paid by the end of the year, and are included in the profit and loss records?

A. Accruals

B. Depreciations

C. Expenses

D. Financial record

Correct Answer: A. Accruals

Explanation: Accruals refer to expenses that have been incurred but not yet paid by the end of the accounting period. These expenses are recognized in the profit and loss statement to accurately reflect the expenses related to that period, even though the actual payment may occur in a later period.

Question 26

True or False: The excess credits (or debits) on the income statement are utilized to decrease (or increase) the equity account.

A. True

B. False

Correct Answer: B. False

Explanation: The excess credits (or debits) on the income statement do not directly impact the equity account. Instead, they contribute to the net income (or loss) for the period, which is then transferred to the equity account through the statement of changes in equity.

Question 27

Skimming schemes often target revenue sources that are difficult to monitor and predict, such as late fees and parking fees. These are considered:

A. Revenue sources

B. Recorded sales

C. Internal audits

D. Register manipulations

Correct Answer: A. Revenue sources

Explanation: Skimming schemes typically target revenue sources because they involve the theft of cash before it is recorded in the accounting system. Revenue sources like late fees and parking fees are often targeted because they involve cash transactions that are not easily monitored or predicted.

Question 28

What factor can make it easier for an employee to skim sales or receivables?

A. Revenue sources and recording procedures

B. Poor collection and recording procedures

C. Internal audits and recording procedures

D. Register manipulations and recording procedures

Correct Answer: B. Poor collection and recording procedures

Explanation: Poor collection and recording procedures can make it easier for an employee to skim sales or receivables because there may be inadequate checks and balances in place to detect and prevent such activities. Without proper oversight, employees may find it easier to manipulate records or siphon off cash without detection.

Question 29

Who is typically responsible for committing financial statement fraud?

A. Organized criminals

B. Mid and lower-level employees

C. Senior management

D. All of the above

Correct Answer: D. All of the above

Explanation: Financial statement fraud can be committed by various individuals or groups within an organization, including organized criminals, mid and lower-level employees, and senior management. Each group may have different motives and opportunities to engage in fraudulent activities related to financial statements.

Question 30

Which approach involves fraudsters creating financial statements of their choice, possibly using only a typewriter or a personal computer?

A. Organized accounting

B. Playing the accounting

C. Beating accounting

D. Outside accounting system

Correct Answer: C. Beating accounting

Explanation: "Beating accounting" refers to a fraudulent approach where individuals produce financial statements using minimal resources, such as a typewriter or a personal computer, to fabricate financial information. This method allows fraudsters to manipulate financial records to their advantage.

Question 31

What is a recommended step to prepare an organization for a formal fraud investigation?

A. Notify all managers about the investigation, explaining its purpose and the individuals involved.

B. Inform key decision-makers when the investigation is about to commence.

C. Send an email to all employees detailing the investigation's purpose.

D. Be sure to inform the subject that they are being investigated.

Correct Answer: B. Inform key decision-makers when the investigation is about to commence.

Explanation: It is important to notify key decision-makers in an organization when a formal fraud investigation is about to begin. This allows them to prepare for any potential impacts the investigation may have on the organization and its operations. It also ensures that relevant stakeholders are aware of the situation and can provide necessary support or information as needed.

Question 32

When a Certified Fraud Examiner (CFE) needs to obtain court records and ensure their accuracy, the most reliable method in most countries is to obtain them directly from court authorities.

A. True

B. False

Correct Answer: A. True

Explanation: Obtaining court records directly from court authorities is generally considered the most reliable method to ensure their accuracy. This approach reduces the risk of receiving altered or falsified documents and helps maintain the integrity of the investigation.

Question 33

A fraud examiner suspects that illicit funds were used to construct a commercial building intended for a restaurant. Which of the following records would be MOST helpful in confirming the owner of the building?

A. Building permit records

B. Commercial filings

C. Voter registration records

D. Local court records

Correct Answer: B. Commercial filings

Explanation: Commercial filings, such as those related to property ownership or business registrations, would be the most helpful in confirming the owner of the building. These records typically provide detailed information about the ownership of commercial properties and can help verify if the suspect is the owner of the building in question.

Question 34

Which of the following options correctly categorizes types of corruption?

A. Conflicts of interest, bribery, unlawful gratuities, and economic extortion

B. Corruption, bribery, economic extortion, conflicts of interest

C. Overbilling, bribery, bid-rigging, and illegal gratuities

D. Economic extortion, bribery, illegal gratuities, and corruption

Correct answer: A. Conflicts of interest, bribery, unlawful gratuities, and economic extortion

Explanation: These are the commonly recognized classifications of corruption. Bribery is the practice of giving or receiving something of value in return for power or obedience or action. Economic extortion is the use of coercion to obtain money or property. Illegal gratuities are similar to bribery but involve offering or accepting something of value after a decision has been made. Conflicts of interest occur when personal interests interfere with professional duties.

Question 35

When an employee uses a fabricated name and address to collect disbursements from fraudulent billing, what is the term for it?

A. Accomplice residence

B. Shell company

C. Perpetrator check

D. Cash generator

Correct answer: B. Shell company

Explanation: A shell company is a type of company that is formed solely for the purpose of creating a façade for illegal activities, such as collecting disbursements from false billings. The fabricated name and post office box are used to make the shell company appear legitimate, but its main function is to facilitate fraudulent transactions.

Question 36

What makes credit card statements valuable in tracing investigations?

A. Credit card records can reveal signs of skimming.

B. Credit card statements offer insights into the subject's litigation history.

C. Credit card statements may list the names of individuals or businesses that the subject transacts business with.

D. Credit card statements display the origin of the funds used to settle a credit card bill.

Correct answer: C. Credit card statements may list the names of individuals or businesses that the subject transacts business with.

Explanation of the correct answer: Credit card statements can be useful in tracing investigations because they can reveal the names of individuals or companies with whom the subject conducts business. This information can be crucial in understanding the subject's financial activities and relationships, which can be helpful in investigative processes.

Question 37

When multiple assets or liabilities of the subject have changed and financial records are unavailable, which method is most effective for tracing assets?

A. Bank deposit method

B. Regression analysis

C. Net worth method

D. Benford's Law analysis

Correct answer: A. Bank deposit method

Explanation of the correct answer: The bank deposit method is the most effective in such scenarios because it involves analyzing the subject's bank deposits to determine the source of funds, which can help trace assets even without access to financial records. This method relies on the assumption that all income is deposited into the bank, making it a useful tool for tracing assets when other methods are not feasible.

Question 38

Which of the following is an uncommon use of public sources of information?

A. Obtaining an individual's credit records

B. Finding out about a person's lifestyle

C. Developing background information on a subject

D. Corroborating or refuting witness statements

Correct answer: A. Obtaining an individual's credit records

Explanation of the correct answer: While public sources of information can be used for various purposes, including finding out about a person's lifestyle, developing background information, and corroborating or refuting witness statements, obtaining an individual's credit records is not typically considered a common use of public sources. Credit records are usually obtained through private and secure channels due to their sensitive nature.

Question 39

What term is used for a continuous count that tracks the expected amount of inventory on hand?

A. Altered inventory

B. Perpetual inventory

C. Shrinking inventory

D. Fictitious inventory

Correct answer: B. Perpetual inventory

Explanation: Perpetual inventory is a system where inventory levels are continuously monitored and recorded, providing a real-time view of stock levels. This helps in maintaining accurate inventory records and enables timely reordering of stock.

Question 40

How can an investigation be conducted discreetly to avoid alerting suspected perpetrators under scrutiny?

A. Investigate during nonbusiness hours.

B. Disclose the investigation to all employees.

C. Terminate the suspected employee.

D. Delay taking any action.

Correct Answer: A. Investigate during nonbusiness hours.

Explanation: Conducting investigations during nonbusiness hours can help avoid alerting suspected perpetrators, as they are less likely to be present or aware of the investigation, allowing for a more discreet process.

Question 41

How can Brice, a Certified Fraud Examiner (CFE), build a connection with Slave, a fraud suspect, during an interview?

A. Establish rapport.

B. Calibrate the witness.

C. Establish the interview theme.

D. Exhibit passive listening.

Correct Answer: A. Establish rapport.

Explanation: Brice's use of humor and casual conversation about a shared experience, such as wearing the same tie, is an attempt to establish rapport with Slave. Building rapport can help create a more comfortable environment for the interview and encourage the suspect to open up and provide more information.

Question 42

When writing fraud examination reports, which audience should be considered?

A. Witnesses

B. Judges or juries

C. Opposing legal counsel

D. All of the above

Correct Answer: D. All of the above

Explanation: Fraud examination reports should be written with all potential audiences in mind, including witnesses, judges or juries, and opposing legal counsel. Reports should be clear, concise, and accurate to effectively communicate findings to these audiences.

Question 43

What is the term for the difference between the physical inventory and perpetual inventory totals?

A. Altered inventory

B. Account receivable

C. Shrinkage

D. Write-offs

Correct answer: C. Shrinkage

Explanation: Shrinkage is the term used to describe the variation between physical inventory (actual inventory count) and perpetual inventory (recorded inventory levels). This difference can be due to theft, damage, errors in recording, or other causes.

Question 44

Which of the following would be most helpful in determining the creation date of a specific document file?

A. The system log

B. Internet activity data

C. The document's metadata

D. Operating system partition

Correct Answer: C. The document's metadata

Explanation: The metadata of a document contains information about the file, including its creation date. This information is typically more reliable for determining the creation date than other sources such as system logs, internet activity data, or the operating system partition.

Question 45

When conducting a fraud examination, a Certified Fraud Examiner (CFE) must proceed as though:

A. There will be a complete internal resolution to the issue

B. The suspect is guilty.

C. The case will end in litigation.

D. The case will end after the suspect is terminated.

Correct Answer: B. The suspect is guilty.

Explanation: In a fraud examination, a CFE must maintain a mindset that the suspect is guilty to ensure a thorough investigation is conducted. This does not imply a presumption of guilt but rather an approach that considers all evidence and possibilities.

Question 46

Which of the following is a common issue related to material and fraud?

A. Misappropriations

B. Civil lawsuit

C. Fraudulent statement

D. Quality control

Correct answer: A. Misappropriations

Explanation: Misappropriations refer to the fraudulent use or theft of funds, assets, or resources for personal gain. This is a common issue in fraud cases where individuals misuse company funds or assets for their own benefit, leading to financial losses for the organization.

Question 47

Which accounting principle ensures that the financial figures presented by a company are not understated and may even be overstated?

A. Fraudulent statement

B. Misappropriations

C. Conservatism

D. Matching

Correct answer: C. Conservatism

Explanation: Conservatism is an accounting principle that guides the preparation of financial statements. It suggests that when in doubt, accountants should choose the option that is least likely to overstate assets or income. This principle ensures that financial figures are at least as much as reflected in the statements, if not more, to avoid misleading investors and stakeholders.

Question 48

Accounting records are primarily based on subjective evidence, not objective evidence:

A. True

B. False

Correct answer: B. False

Explanation: Accounting records are designed to be kept on objective evidence, not subjective evidence. Objective evidence includes documents like receipts, invoices, and bank statements, which provide factual support for the transactions recorded in the accounting records. Keeping records based on objective evidence helps ensure the accuracy and reliability of financial information.

Question 49

When is revenue recognized?

A. Realized and Earned

B. Fictitious and Earned

C. Realized and Evidenced

D. All of the above

Correct answer: A. Realized and Earned

Explanation: Revenue is recognized when it is both realized (meaning the company has received payment or expects to receive payment) and earned (meaning the company has provided goods or services to the customer). This recognition typically occurs at the point of sale or when the service is performed, depending on the nature of the transaction and the accounting method used.

Question 50

Which of the following is NOT a motive for bribing employees of the purchaser?

A. For late bids to be received

B. To extend the bid opening date

C. To ensure bid-splitting

D. To falsify the bid log

Correct Answer: C. To ensure bid-splitting

Explanation: Bid-splitting is an unethical practice that involves dividing a contract into smaller parts to avoid competitive bidding, thereby reducing competition and potentially inflating prices. It is illegal and undermines the integrity of the bidding process.

www.ingramcontent.com/pod-product-compliance
Lightning Source LLC
Chambersburg PA
CBHW081021240526
45471CB00018B/3934